D1241422

# THE WORLD OF MUSIC

EDITED BY SIR GEORGE FRANCKENSTEIN, G.C.V.O., AND OTTO ERICH DEUTSCH

## COVENT GARDEN

JOHN RICH AS HARLEQUIN

*Water-colour by an unknown artist, 1753*

DESMOND
SHAWE-TAYLOR

# COVENT GARDEN

*WITH 7 PLATES IN COLOUR*
*& 28 BLACK-AND-WHITE*
*ILLUSTRATIONS*

NEW YORK

CHANTICLEER PRESS

FIRST PUBLISHED 1948 BY

CHANTICLEER PRESS INC 41 EAST 50TH STREET NEW YORK

IN ASSOCIATION WITH

ADPRINT LTD LONDON

792
S537c
91024

PRINTED IN HOLLAND
BY NEDERLANDSCHE ROTOGRAVURE LEIDEN

# CONTENTS

# PLATES IN COLOUR

# ILLUSTRATIONS IN BLACK & WHITE

*I am indebted to Dr. Loewenberg for reading my proofs and offering much valuable advice ; to Professor Dent, Mr. Hurtley and the staff of the Gabrielle Enthoven Collection for placing at my disposal their time and their specialised knowledge ; and to many others whom I cannot name for lack of space.*

D. S.-T.

To SYBIL JACKSON

IN GRATITUDE FOR MY FIRST, AND BEST, 'ROSENKAVALIER'

MAY 12, 1927

The Editors wish to thank the following for permission to reproduce the pictures
in this book: Colour: Frontispiece and page 20, the Garrick Club; page
37, the Director of the Victoria & Albert Museum; page 38, Mr.
Oliver Messel; page 55, Mr. Gerald Corcoran; page 56, Mr.
Leslie Hurry.   Black-and-White: On the following pages:
13, 30, 31, 53, the Covent Garden Opera Trust;
24, 25, the City Librarian, Birmingham; 33, 41,
45, the Illustrated London News and the
London Electrotype Agency Ltd.; 47, the
Trustees of the Tate Gallery; 51,
Messrs. John Lane, The Bodley
Head Ltd.; 67, Mr. Robin
Ironside; 68, the Bri-
tish Council; 71,
Mr. William
Chappell

The Masque at the Old House

*THE FIRST THEATRE: 1732–1808*

I

## A MISCELLANY OF DRAMATIC ENTERTAINMENT

CCORDING to Sir Thomas Browne, who had an almost Chestertonian vein of paradox, it is "not so great a miracle that there was a deluge once as that there is not one always". The theatrical historian comes to entertain a similar view about the fires which so punctually consumed the playhouses of London. What with wooden scenery, muslin transformation drops, guttering candles, back-stage draughts, the inadequacy of the extinguishing devices and the irregularity of the fire service, Covent Garden did well, maybe, to have no more than two fires in the two centuries of its theatrical history; and indeed we must count ourselves fortunate that the third theatre on this site should have survived the incendiary raids of the recent war.

During the eighteenth century and the first half of the nineteenth, the principal London home of opera and ballet was the King's Theatre in the Haymarket. Covent Garden did not become a fully-fledged opera house until the last decade of its second theatre, just a hundred years ago; before that time it generally presented a miscellany of dramatic entertainment in which music played either an accessory part, or none at all. A mainly musical chronicle such as this cannot do more than glance at the history of the legitimate drama; the play, on this occasion, is *not* the thing, and I shall offer no further apology for the indecent speed at which the mighty ghosts of Garrick, Kemble and Mrs. Siddons must seem to flit across the page.

The name of Covent Garden derives from a nunnery once attached to the Abbey of Westminster. The first of the three theatres which have occupied this "convent" site was built by John Rich. Rich had succeeded to letters patent, originally granted to Sir William Davenant by Charles II, to build a theatre anywhere in London, wherein "tragedies, comedies, plays, operas, musick, scenes and all other entertainments of the stage whatsoever, may be shown and presented". He was already manager of the successful theatre at Lincoln's Inn Fields, and is now remembered principally for his connexion with *The Beggar's Opera*; as everybody knows, it was this work which "made Gay rich, and Rich gay". John Rich might be described as the English equivalent of Emanuel Schikaneder (the librettist and first Papageno of Mozart's *Magic Flute*). He has some claim to be considered the inventor of English pantomime, and under the stage name of Lun was famous in the part of Harlequin, which—as we learn from Garrick's description—he acted in dumb show:

> When Lun appeared, with matchless art and whim
> He gave the power of speech to every limb;
> Tho' masked and mute, conveyed his quick intent,
> And told in frolic gesture what he meant.

There is an early etching of him in this character, and a contemporary description of the "business" in which he indulged in a scene during which Harlequin is hatched from an egg by the heat of the sun, "from the first chirping in the egg, his receiving motion, his feeling of the ground, standing upright, to his quick trip round the empty shell". He was illiterate (in *Roderick Random* Smollett lampooned him as Vandal); and in private life he was addicted to the company of cats (of which at one time he had 27), of wives (of whom, in succession, he married three) and—if Fielding and Pope are to be believed—of concubines as well.

In spite of all these distractions, and those attendant on the management of a great theatre, he found time to inaugurate a once celebrated club known as "The Sublime Society of Beefsteaks". From 1735 onwards many of the most eminent men of the day would assemble in his room at Covent Garden for conversation and the consumption of steaks dressed by Rich himself. The club survived his death, and maintained its connexion with Covent Garden until 1808, when its entire stock of wines was destroyed in the fire of that year. Thereafter it migrated to the old Lyceum, and did not finally close its doors until 1867.

In Rich's time the Covent Garden site was not considered very eligible,

RICH'S GLORY *or his* Triumphant Entry *into* Covent-Garden.

JOHN RICH TAKES POSSESSION OF COVENT GARDEN
Rich in the carriage, John Gay borne aloft in front
*Cartoon attributed to William Hogarth, 1732*

and he was able to secure it at a ground rent of £100 a year. The building which he erected on this site as a neighbour and rival to Drury Lane seems to have been quite a small one. Unlike the two later theatres, it had no frontage on Bow Street, but was approached by means of a narrow colonnade; and its stage, according to Northcott, was about 20 feet wide and 47 feet deep, and lighted by four hoops bearing candles.

The new theatre was opened on December 7, 1732, with a revival of Congreve's *Way of the World*, and it is interesting to recall the prices which then obtained. 5s. was charged for admission to the boxes (of which there were fifty-five), 2s. 6d. to the pit, 2s. and 1s. to the gallery, and 10s. for a seat on the stage; "servants", a later play-bill tells us, "will be allowed to keep places on the stage, and the ladies are desired to send them by 3 o'clock". Although at these rates the house was calculated to hold £200, only £115 was actually taken on the first night. But an early revival of *The Beggar's Opera* put the theatre firmly on the theatrical map, and it became particularly popular in Court circles for the curious reason that there was direct access from the Royal Box to the green-room, so that noble patrons were not obliged to cross the stage, as at Drury Lane, under the inquisitive eyes of their inferiors.

Like all English theatres of the eighteenth and nineteenth centuries, Covent Garden frequently presented "mixed bills" of the most variegated order. In 1734, for example, we find *The Way of the World* followed by miscellaneous "entertainments of dancing", the final item being "a new dance called *Pigmalion*, performed by Mr. Malter and Mlle Sallé". This was an occasion of some moment in the history of ballet, being the first on which a ballerina had the courage to discard the towering perukes and swelling panniers of French court tradition in favour of a simple Greek robe of muslin.

But the musical importance of the first theatre consists almost entirely in its association with Handel, which lasted intermittently from 1734 to his death in 1759. It was after the failure of the second of his two Haymarket ventures that Handel transferred his attention to Covent Garden. He began with a revival of *Pastor Fido*: but the first of his operas newly composed for Covent Garden was *Ariodante* (1735), which was followed later in the same year by the more fortunate *Alcina*; in 1736 *Atalanta* was produced with particularly lavish scenery, and in 1737 no less than three operas, *Arminio*, *Giustino* and *Berenice*, of which none did well and the last quite dashed his hopes of a solid Covent Garden success.

In 1741, after a few more unsuccessful productions at the King's Theatre and Lincoln's Inn Fields, Handel resigned himself to the failure of his operatic career and began to devote all his energy to the development of that successful innovation, the Handelian oratorio. These works are in many respects not unlike the operas; but they soon endeared themselves to a large public by their English texts, their familiar biblical narratives and their massively effective use of the chorus. The first London performance of *Messiah* in 1743, in the presence of George II, set the seal on Handel's success in this new venture; and thereafter it became the custom to give a dozen or so oratorio performances at Covent Garden every Lent: a custom which continued almost without interruption until the composer's death in 1759—and for long afterwards.

Apart from the Lenten oratorios, Covent Garden had reverted, since the failure of the Handel operas, to the production of straight plays. In 1738 Shakespeare was honoured by a long series of elaborate representations, and from time to time a limited number of Restoration plays were revived; but most of the other productions of the period were of ephemeral interest. There was a curious fashion for the performance by actresses of what were known as "breeches parts": thus Captain Macheath, in *The Beggar's Opera*, was frequently played by women, among them the fascinating Peg Woffing-

LUIGI MARCHESI, A MALE SOPRANO
who sang at Covent Garden
*Engraving after Richard Cosway, 1790*

ton, who also shone (strange as it may seem) as the outrageous Sir Harry Wildair in Farquhar's *Constant Couple*. It was one of her performances in this role which prompted that celebrated back-stage *riposte* attributed by Tate Wilkinson to Kitty Clive. "I believe", said Peg with complacency, "that one half of the audience took me for a man." "Do not be uneasy," replied her rival; "you are satisfied the other half know the contrary."

The first actor of immortal renown to appear at Covent Garden was David Garrick, who played a round of his principal parts there in 1746; a year later he bought Drury Lane, where he reigned for the best part of thirty years. It was at Covent Garden, however, that he appeared in the same play as the veteran James Quin, thus provoking a direct comparison between the old and the new styles of acting. The play was Rowe's *Fair Penitent*; and Richard Cumberland, the future dramatist, then a scholar in the sixth form at Westminster, who had obtained a seat in the front row of the gallery, has left us a famous description of the occasion:

> Quin . . . in an enormous full-bottomed periwig . . . with very little variation of cadence, and in a deep full tone, accompanied by a sawing kind of action which had more of the senate than of the stage in it . . . rolled out his heroics with an air of dignified indifference that seemed to disdain the plaudits that were bestowed upon him. . . . When, after a long and eager expectation, I first beheld little Garrick, then young and light and active in every muscle and feature, come bounding on the stage—Heavens, what a transition! It seemed as if a whole century had been stept over in the passage of a single scene.

Two years after the death of Handel, that is to say in 1761, Rich died, and the management of his theatre passed into the hands of his two sons-in-law, of whom the more important was John Beard, an admirable singer for whom Handel had composed many of the great tenor parts in his oratorios. As might have been expected, Beard specialised in musical productions, and one of his first and most elaborate was Dr. Arne's *Artaxerxes*. This was an attempt to write an English opera in the fully-composed Italian style, with arias and recitatives, and to a libretto translated from Metastasio by the composer; it had some success in its day, but the style never caught on. "Like many English composers," says Professor Dent, "Arne was a generation behind his time; the sort of opera which he wanted to write was already dying out everywhere." After *Artaxerxes* we hear no more of "Anglo-Italian opera", but find ourselves in the midst of those innumerable pastiches and ballad operas which were to form the staple operatic fare of the British public for the best part of a century; the most famous of the composers and "arrangers" of these pieces were Arne and Dibdin in the eighteenth century, and Sir Henry Bishop in the early nineteenth.

The decadence of both drama and music in England during this period may be fairly attributed to the fact that they were continually getting in one another's way; audiences, far from being indifferent to music, were so crazy about it that (to the great annoyance of the dramatists) they insisted on the constant interpolation of songs into plays; on the other hand, in spite of the success of *Artaxerxes*, the public (or perhaps one should say the composers) would never take the decisive step towards full-blooded opera with music from the beginning to the end. Later in the century, when the new *opera buffa* was sweeping through Europe, we remained obstinately uncertain of the dividing line between comic opera and comedy-with-songs;

THE PIAZZA, COVENT GARDEN, IN 1768
Looking towards the entrance of the first Theatre
*Coloured engraving by Edward Rooker after Thomas Sandby*

nor was the sphere of the composer at all well defined at Covent Garden:
the famous tenor John Braham, for example, was for many years accustomed
to write the music himself for his own parts.

In the 1760's and 1770's Goldsmith and Sheridan were the great names
at Covent Garden; but apart from the latter's *Duenna* their careers belong
to theatrical rather than to musical history. About this time the shadow of
Mozart begins to be felt in two small episodes. In 1777 a small girl of 11,
named Nancy Storace, appeared during the oratorio season; nine years later
she was to be the first Susanna at Vienna. And in 1784 a version of Beau-
marchais's *Marriage of Figaro* was put on at Covent Garden in the oddest
circumstances. The text had not yet been printed, and all manuscript copies
were jealously guarded by the French managers. So the Covent Garden
playwright Holcroft visited Paris and went, along with a French friend, to
eight or nine performances in succession "until they were able to write out
the plot and some of the dialogue with sufficient exactness". In spite of its
Continental success, the opera based on this play did not reach London

until 1812 (Haymarket, in Italian) and was not given at Covent Garden until 1819—and then only in an English "adaptation" by Bishop. But though we may have been slow to discover the operas of Mozart, their popularity and staying-power proved greater in England than in France or Italy; according to Dr. Loewenberg, the ever delightful *Entführung aus dem Serail* was not given anywhere in Italy until 1935.

Two extraordinary theatrical occasions distinguished the 1780's. On February 28, 1786, Mrs. Siddons made her first appearance at Covent Garden, as Belvidera in Otway's *Venice Preserved*; and on May 7, 1789, Charles Macklin chose for his farewell appearance his most famous role of Shylock, being by that time not less than 90; indeed, if the tablet erected to his memory by his widow in St. Paul's Church is to be believed, he must have been 99! Up till a year or two previously his memory had remained unimpaired; but on this melancholy occasion the poor old man could do no more than begin the play, apologise for his forgetfulness, and retire. Nevertheless he survived for another eight years.

In the summer recess of 1792 the theatre was largely rebuilt at a reputed cost of £25,000, the interior being redecorated mainly in green and gold; a certain Thomas Harris, who had long been a part-owner, was responsible for the ambitious renovation. To recover some of his outlay he unwisely decided to abolish the shilling gallery: a step which led to one more of those many riots which recur throughout English theatrical history well into the reign of Queen Victoria. Thirty years before, disgraceful scenes had taken place during Arne's *Artaxerxes* because of the refusal of the management to admit the public at half-price after the third act. There is little doubt that our playhouse manners were among the rowdiest in Europe; the *locus classicus* for the appalling impression they made, as late as the 1820's, on a cultivated foreigner is the correspondence of Prince Pückler-Muskau, some extracts from which were published by Professor Dent in his recent entertaining history of the Old Vic and Sadler's Wells. How, one wonders, did the great players of the day contrive to make their effect amid such pandemonium? In 1801, during a performance of *Richard III*, a drunken galleryite threw a quart bottle at a minor actor named Betterton, and the ensuing uproar was not quelled, nor the play enabled to proceed, until the appearance of five guardsmen with fixed bayonets in the gallery. Five years later, an apple, supposed to have been aimed at some people behaving noisily in a box, flew perilously close to Mrs. Siddons herself during *Coriolanus*, and the incident led to a spirited protest by her brother, the great John Philip Kemble. Such were the conditions (not everyday perhaps, but

A RIOT DURING A PERFORMANCE OF 'ARTAXERXES'
The manager refused to admit late-comers to the pit at half-price
*Engraved cartoon, 1763*

of fairly frequent occurrence) at almost every theatre in London with the exception of the Italian Opera in the Haymarket.

During the 1790's Gothic tendencies become evident in such play-titles as *Fontainville Forest, The Sicilian Romance* (after Mrs. Radcliffe) and *The Mysteries of the Castle.* The Lenten oratorios, under John Ashley, were beginning to degenerate into musical variety entertainments, and a concerto or two would be cheerfully interpolated into performances of *The Messiah.* Nevertheless some important novelties were given at Covent Garden for the first time in England, including Haydn's *Creation* in 1800 and Mozart's *Requiem* the following year. In 1803 Kemble acquired a share in the ownership and control of the theatre; his first season was notable for the mounting of no fewer than eleven of Shakespeare's plays, and his second for the furore caused by the boy actor known as Master Betty, or "the infant Roscius" In 1805 the capital comedian Charles Mathews first appeared at Covent Garden, and in the following year the immortal clown Grimaldi made his début: immortal, if only because his Christian name Giuseppe (*anglice* Joey) has become the generic name for all clowns.

On the night of September 20, 1808, Sheridan's *Pizarro* was played. This forgotten tragedy calls for the discharge of a gun; and it has been conjectured that a piece of smouldering wadding from this gun may have caused the fire which broke out at four o'clock the following morning. Whatever its origin, it raged almost unchecked; by six o'clock the interior was gutted and the roof had fallen. Everything was lost: scenery, costumes, armour, jewellery, playbooks; the huge collection of printed and manuscript music, and Handel's organ, which he had bequeathed to Rich at his death, and which can be discerned in the Pugin-Rowlandson aquatint below. To crown the disaster, some twenty-five persons lost their lives in attempting to fight the flames. For the Kemble family it was a crippling blow, and one from which, despite the generous contributions received from all sides towards the rebuilding fund, they were never wholly to recover.

PERFORMANCE OF AN ORATORIO
At Covent Garden before the fire of 1808
*Coloured aquatint by Pugin and Rowlandson*

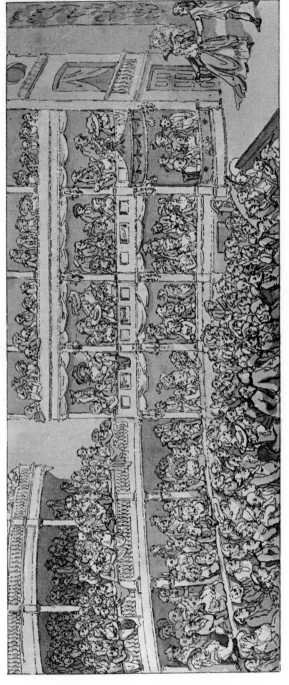

INTERIOR OF THE FIRST THEATRE, COVENT GARDEN
*Coloured aquatint by Thomas Rowlandson, 1786*

PEG WOFFINGTON
Painting by an unknown artist, c. 1745–1755

II

# FROM THEATRE TO OPERA HOUSE

N 1808 important buildings were planned and completed a great deal
more rapidly than they are to-day. Three months after the destruction
of the old theatre, on December 12, 1808, the foundation stone of
its successor was laid by the Prince Regent—a stone which has been
preserved in the structure of the present building. The theatre reopened its
doors on September 18, 1809—less than twelve months after the fire—with
a performance of *Macbeth* "to which will be added the Musical Entertainment
of *The Quaker*". In the intervening period (on February 24) Drury Lane
had also been burnt to the ground, and was not to reopen until 1812.

The new Covent Garden, designed by Sir Robert Smirke, was a considerably larger building than the old; in fact, it was one of the largest
theatres in Europe. It had a frontage in Bow Street, ornamented with a
fine portico; the width of its proscenium was 42 feet 6 inches, some eight
feet wider than that of the present theatre; and after certain modifications
the auditorium accommodated 2,800 persons (not counting the occupants
of the private boxes), which is considerably more than the present capacity.
These modifications were the direct result of the famous O.P. ("old prices")
riots, which began on the opening night and raged for nearly three months.
The trouble was simply the increase of prices for seats in the public boxes
from six to seven shillings; and at first sight the organised ruffianism to
which it gave rise seems to us no more than what Cobbett called it, "an
attempt to compel people to sell entertainment at the price pointed out by
the purchasers". But Fitzgerald, in his *Lives of the Kembles*, is careful to
remind us that Drury Lane and Covent Garden, "by their patents and
established position, had almost a monopoly of the theatrical amusements
of the town": in modern terms, although quite unsubsidised, the patent
theatres were in effect national institutions.

But whatever the justice of their case, the rioters stopped at nothing
in their demonstrations. "When the performers entered," says Dibdin, "they
were greeted with applause, to indicate that what would follow was not
meant personally to them; but the instant they attempted to speak,
'Off! off!', overpowering hisses, appalling hoots, and the 'O.P. Dance'

commenced, in which the whole audience joined. The dance was performed with deliberate and ludicrous gravity, each person pronouncing the letters 'O.P.' as loud as he could, and accompanying the pronunciation of each with a beat, or blow on the floor or seat beneath him with his feet, a stick, or a bludgeon, and as the numerous performers kept in strict time and unison with each other, it was one of the most whimsically tantalising banters or torments that could be conceived."

All official and legal attempts to quell the disturbances failed; whereupon Kemble and his colleagues ill-advisedly took the law into their own hands by engaging "Dutch Sam" and other professional pugilists to go into the pit and fight the mob. Feeling against the Kembles hereupon rose so high that, according to Mrs. Siddons, Mrs. Kemble was obliged to live "poor soul . . . with ladders at her windows, in order to make her escape through the garden in case of an attack". The affair ended in total defeat for the proprietors; Kemble himself met three hundred of his leading enemies at dinner at the Crown and Anchor Tavern (one of the oddest imaginable occasions for a feast) and agreed to all their demands; he was even forced to apologise in his theatre for having employed "improper persons" (*i.e.* Dutch Sam and Co.). Whereupon the rioters hoisted a placard from the pit carrying the words "We are satisfied"; and apart from a misguided attempt on the part of Kemble to evade some of the conditions at the beginning of the following season, the disgraceful affair was over. While it lasted, it provided society and the press with a controversial topic of the first order.

One of the conditions of Kemble's capitulation was the abolition of the twenty-six private boxes on the third tier—a step which was said to have cost him over £10,000 a year. To recover his losses he began to put on pantomimes of a spectacular kind; in one of these, *Bluebeard,* among other attractions sixteen mounted Spahis were to be seen "ascending the heights with inconceivable velocity"; in another the boards of Covent Garden were trodden, for the first time, by an elephant. Severe critics have been shocked at such sensationalism, but pantomimes had from the first been a part of the Covent Garden tradition, and they continued to flourish every Christmas long after the theatre had acquired the dignified title of the Royal Italian Opera. Saxe Wyndham tells a curious story of the Christmas season of 1810, in which Grimaldi was appearing in both the Sadler's Wells and the Covent Garden pantomimes, the one coming first in the evening's entertainments, the other last. A cab was held in readiness to transport him from stage to stage, but one night it failed to appear, and the Clerkenwell population was astonished to observe the conscientious clown running full

FAÇADE OF THE SECOND THEATRE, COVENT GARDEN
As rebuilt by Sir Robert Smirke after the fire of 1808
*Coloured aquatint by Benwell and Reeve, 1809*

tilt in his motley through the streets: a scene which nearly led to a riot.

In the season of 1811-12 Mrs. Siddons took formal leave of the stage in a round of her principal roles, terminating in a triumphant Lady Macbeth on June 29, 1812. But as so often happens in the theatrical world, this proved to be not "positively" her farewell appearance, which took place on June 9, 1819, in Home's *Douglas*. Her brother also went into a temporary retirement from which he emerged in 1814, when the tremendous success of Edmund Kean at Drury Lane caused much anxiety at the rival house. Two years later Covent Garden played a trump card in the engagement of Charles Macready; and for some years the two great tragedians divided the allegiance of the town between the two theatres. The departure of Kemble (his farewell appearance, as Coriolanus, took place on June 23, 1817) and Macready's magnificent Richard III of 1819 consolidated the latter's position as the leading Covent Garden actor.

During this period the theatre underwent a diminution of popularity which not even the success of Macready could wholly counteract. The original building debt, with its load of interest, proved a perpetual encumbrance; and the death in 1820 of Thomas Harris, patentee and chief proprietor, seems to have prompted Kemble, now in retirement at Toulouse, to make over his own share in the ownership to his brother Charles. Between the latter and Henry Harris (who succeeded his father) relations became strained; and an open quarrel led to the retirement of Henry Harris in 1822. It is impossible in a brief history to trace all the ramifications of ownership and management which occurred during the next quarter of a century; but generally speaking the theatre continued to be ill run, and in 1831 it was involved in no fewer than six lawsuits. The migration of Kean to Covent Garden for the last five years of his life ought to have helped matters; though already a victim to the brandy-drinking which brought his career to a premature end, he remained an incomparable performer almost to the last. But no artistic success could mend the fortunes of a management so reckless in the distribution of free seats (in a period of less than two months no fewer than 11,083 "orders" were said to have been written out by the treasurer); and by 1829 the theatre was bankrupt.

From this chronicle of disturbance and financial anxiety it is a relief to turn to the musical episodes in the theatre's history; being episodes only, they seem to stand apart from the main stream of intrigue, jealousy and incompetence. In 1810 Mr. Henry Bishop, one-time apprentice jockey in a Newmarket racing stable, and the future knight and composer of "Home, Sweet Home", was appointed musical director. In accordance with the taste of his day, his task was to provide incidental music (largely unnecessary, according to our ideas) for a long series of Shakespearian revivals, and to "adapt" for the English stage the operatic masterpieces of Mozart, Rossini, Boïeldieu and Auber: it seemed impossible at that time to present any

'THE LIBERTINE': AN ADAPTATION OF MOZART'S 'DON GIOVANNI' AT COVENT GARDEN
John Chapman as the Commandant, Anne Mathews as Donna Anna, John Sinclair as Don Octavio
*Toy Theatre Sheet, 1817*

'The Libertine': an Adaptation of Mozart's 'Don Giovanni' at Covent Garden
Charles Kemble as Don Juan, John Liston as Lepeorello
*Toy Theatre Sheet, 1817*

foreign opera without a quantity of interpolations and "additional music".

Weber's *Der Freischütz* was one of the most immediate and widespread successes of operatic history; it reached even our own notoriously laggard capital in 1824, only three years after its first production; and in that year it was given, more or less simultaneously and in various adaptations, in no fewer than four theatres: the Lyceum, the Surrey, Covent Garden and Drury Lane. The last had "additional music" by Bishop, who had now changed theatres; and he was to be succeeded at Covent Garden by no less a musician than Weber himself, who had been persuaded by Charles Kemble to write a new opera specially for his theatre, and to come over to produce and conduct it in person.

Although suffering from a mortal consumption, Weber put all his strength into the work of composition. He had agreed enthusiastically to the subject of *Oberon*, based on Wieland's popular fairy epic, but he was much distressed to discover the lukewarm, half-and-half traditions of English opera. He received Planché's libretto piecemeal, and was expected to set it as it arrived, without even knowing the position of the particular piece in the creaking mechanism of the plot. "The cut of an English opera", he gently complains in a letter to his librettist, "is very different from a German one: the English is more or less a drama with songs"; and again, "the intermixing of so many principal actors who do not sing, the omission of the music in the most important moments—all deprive our *Oberon* of the title of an opera, and will make him unfit for all other theatres in Europe". In reply, Planché stressed the importance of conciliating English operatic taste, and exclaimed after the first performance, "Next time we will show them what we can really do."

But there was no "next time", for within two months of the first night Weber was found dead in his bed, at the age of thirty-nine. The first performance of *Oberon*, on April 12, 1826, had been a considerable success, and the composer received a heartening ovation on taking his position at the conductor's desk. But although given thirty-one times in the first season, and frequently revived, it was eventually killed by its idiotic story : a fact which justifies Sir Donald Tovey's savage remark that Weber "poured his last and finest music into this pig-trough, and shared the applause with the magnificent scenery". The only bright spot in this melancholy episode in our operatic history is the total failure of Bishop's *Aladdin*, the feeble counter-attraction to *Oberon* put on at Drury Lane.

The repertory at the Italian Opera in the Haymarket had come to consist in the 1820's largely of Mozart and Rossini, and in the next decade the latter's enormous vogue had penetrated to Covent Garden also, where *La Cenerentola* and *La Gazza Ladra* were given in English versions—no doubt considerably adapted, though perhaps less so than his *Mosè in Egitto*, which was actually interspersed, in 1833, with choruses from Handel's oratorio on the same subject.

During this season Alfred Bunn was joint manager of Covent Garden and Drury Lane; and for some reason the fascinating singer Maria Malibran deserted the Haymarket during the latter years of her brief career to appear under Bunn's management at both theatres, and still more curiously to sing in English as well as in Italian: she was the first English Leonora in Beethoven's *Fidelio*. She died in Manchester, at the very height of her fame, in 1836, and soon became a legend of the early Romantic period; so that it is truly astonishing to learn that her elder brother, the famous singing-teacher Manuel Garcia, survived until 1906.

Bunn used to economise by using as many as possible of his artists for both theatres, sometimes with ludicrous results. Once an impatient Drury Lane audience had to be told that the Scottish tenor, John Templeton, was at that instant completing his performance at Covent Garden with Madame Malibran, and "if the audience would kindly permit the orchestra to repeat the overture, no doubt shortly Mr. Templeton would be in attendance".

MARIA FELICITÀ MALIBRAN
As Desdemona in Rossini's 'Otello'
*Mezzotint after Henri Decaisne, 1836*

When Templeton arrived he was bathed in perspiration, and refused to go on as Masaniello until he could get his whiskers and moustache to stick. In the middle of an aria the offending moustache worked itself into his mouth and when the singer flung it away in a fury, it clung "like an octopus" to the strings of the first violin: an effect which caused the house to rise in a body and cheer. As a rule, however, Templeton possessed a phlegmatic nature, and it is said that to obtain from him the appearance of jealous rage Malibran would occasionally resort to a fierce but surreptitious pinch.

Bunn's cheese-paring ingenuities, however, were unable to solve his financial predicament, and an effort which he made to induce the Government to subsidise the two patent theatres proved to be rather more than a hundred years ahead of its time; at all events Sir Robert Peel dismissed the suggestion in a reply of six lines. The theatre thereafter passed under other managements, including that of Mr. Fitzball, the self-styled "Victor Hugo of England", who is chiefly notable for having obtained, on the occasion of his benefit, the services of Lola Montez—a purely gratuitous action on the dancer's part, as she seems never to have met the worthy manager either before or after this single occasion. Mr. Fitzball, for his part, was fairly stunned by her charms. "I have seen sylphs appear, and female forms of the most dazzling beauty, in ballets and fairy dreams, but the most dazzling and perfect form I ever did gaze upon was Lola Montez, in her splendid white-and-gold attire studded with diamonds."

Macready's connexion with the theatre ended in 1839, when Charles James Mathews (the younger) took his place. His wife, Madame Vestris, was a woman of great versatility, successful alike as manager, singer and actress; among her most celebrated roles were such male charmers as Don Giovanni and Captain Macheath, and the *Beggar's Opera* was accordingly once more revived with its invariable success. The following year *A Midsummer Night's Dream* was given for the first time with Mendelssohn's overture, and in 1845 the *Antigone* of Sophocles with a score by the same composer, who was amused by the circumstances of its production and "laughed for three days", so he said, at a *Punch* cartoon of the choristers. Mendelssohn's name reminds us that we are now in the Victorian age. The young Queen herself, naturally fond of the pleasures of music and the theatre, paid a state visit in the first year of her reign, but the occasion was unfortunate. An enormous mob packed the cheaper seats, causing such tumult, fainting and screaming that "a great number of women had to be lifted over the boxes in an exhausted condition".

In 1843 Drury Lane and Covent Garden lost the monopoly of serious drama which they had enjoyed since 1660; and about the same time Lumley, the manager of the King's Theatre (by this time known as Her Majesty's), began to find himself in those "serious difficulties" which seem inseparable from operatic management in this country. Both he and his immediate predecessor Laporte are said to have devoted more attention to ballet than to opera; at any rate by 1846 dissatisfaction with the Haymarket operatic performances was becoming general, stimulated (as Professor Dent suggests) by the unfavourable comparisons made by returned tourists, who had become a far more frequent class since Waterloo. Nevertheless, when Michael Costa left Her Majesty's in 1846 (where since 1833 he had been musical director and conductor), the musical world was amazed, and at first incredulous, on hearing that all the best remaining singers of the company (with the

COVENT GARDEN: THE SECOND THEATRE
As rebuilt after the fire of 1808
*Coloured aquatint by Pugin and Rowlandson from 'The Microcosm of London'*

single exception of the great *basso* Lablache) had decided to follow him to "a new theatre for foreign musical performances" to be opened in the following season.

The "new theatre" was Covent Garden, which had been totally reconstructed by an architect named Albano, and a prospectus was issued promising "a more perfect representation of the lyric drama than has yet been attained in this country". Not only Grisi, Mario and Tamburini (three of the famous *Don Pasquale* "quartet") but a great part of the orchestra seceded with Costa (they were nicknamed "the Costa-mongers"); and they were joined by a number of almost equally distinguished newcomers, including the soprano Persiani (whose husband had a share in the Covent Garden management), the versatile baritone Ronconi, and that most luscious of contraltos and only pupil of Rossini, Marietta Alboni. The theatre was opened for the first time as the "Royal Italian Opera House" on April 6,

ALESSANDRO TAMBURINI
As Riccardo in 'I Puritani', by Bellini
*Lithograph after Alfred Edward Chalon, 1836*

1847; the opera chosen was Rossini's *Semiramide*, with Grisi, Alboni and Tamburini in the principal roles.

The repertory for the first season consisted of three operas by Bellini, four by Donizetti, three by Mozart, five by Rossini, and two (*I Due Foscari* and *Ernani*) by the newcomer Verdi, whose music was thought (and with some justification) crude and violent by the refined taste of the day, but was nevertheless beginning to make its way with the general public by virtue of its sheer animal vigour. Among the ballets the name of *Manon Lescaut* (afterwards famous as the subject of two operas) strikes the eye; and among the dancers that of Fanny Elssler. Carlotta Grisi did not follow her cousin, the great soprano, to Covent Garden, but remained faithful to Her Majesty's, where she was joined this year for the first time by Marie

GIULIA GRISI
As Desdemona in Rossini's 'Otello'
*Lithograph after Alfred Edward Chalon, 1836*

Taglioni. On the vocal side, however, Lumley would have been poorly off but for the heaven-sent arrival of Jenny Lind, the "Swedish Nightingale". Her immense success and the subsequent return of another great *prima donna*, Henriette Sontag, enabled him to keep things going for a few years; so that from 1847 to 1852 London possessed two rival theatres, both devoted to Italian opera.

It was the second season of the new house which put its artistic success beyond doubt: both musically and scenically the Haymarket opera was outclassed. Works like Donizetti's *La Favorita* and Meyerbeer's *Les Huguenots*, neither of which had previously found favour in England, were launched on their popularity by the imposing *mise-en-scène* in which they were now presented; Malibran's equally wonderful sister, Pauline Viardot-Garcia, the idol of Berlioz and Turgenev, made a triumphant début; and Costa had under him an orchestra of no fewer than eighty players, including sixty-one strings—an unheard-of luxury for those days, and handsome enough for most purposes even to-day. It is perhaps not surprising that Delafield, the wealthy amateur who footed the bill, should have gone bankrupt by the end of the 1849 season; but in England there is generally someone willing to risk bankruptcy for the sake of opera, and he was immediately succeeded by Frederick Beale, who scored a great success with Meyerbeer's *Le Prophète*, in which Pauline Viardot-Garcia created a sensation as Fidès.

Next year, a name famous in the theatre's annals turns up for the first time, when Frederick Gye took over the management. He was a better business man than musician, and it was perhaps fortunate for him that the first period of his management should have coincided with Verdi's great pair of successes, *Rigoletto* and *Il Trovatore*, both of which he was astute enough to bring out only two years after their Italian *premières*. Among his other novelties was Spohr's *Faust* (produced "at the urgent wish of the Queen"), but neither this nor the same composer's *Jessonda* really caught on, while the single performance of Berlioz's *Benvenuto Cellini*, which was conducted by the composer in 1853, was perhaps the most unmitigated fiasco in the history of the English operatic stage.

But in spite of ups and downs the Gye régime prospered. "The appearance of the opera prospectus", said the *Illustrated London News* in 1851, "is anticipated with as much curiosity as a speech from the Throne. . . . No novel of Bulwer or Charles Dickens, no protocol of Palmerston, no manifesto of the Germanic Diet is perused with more avidity." The seasons were a great deal more extended than those we knew before the late war; five months was the average, the 1851 season, for instance, running from April 3 to August 30. On the occasion of the Queen's state visit to *The Magic Flute* in that year, the Grand Foyer was turned into her retiring room: "at each extremity of this saloon, crystal curtains, intermingled with ruby drops, most brilliantly lighted up with gas, were suspended, and large mirrors were placed in every panel."

In 1852 Lumley gave up the unequal struggle, and for the next four years Covent Garden had no rival but Drury Lane, which in the world of opera never enjoyed the same prestige. The legendary *basso cantante*, Lablache, was now free to rejoin his colleagues; and in 1855 the old *Don Pasquale* quartet was once again, and for the last time, reunited in several performances of Donizetti's delicious masterpiece.

Between opera seasons, Covent Garden was accustomed to house many other forms of entertainment, of which the most important were the famous Promenade Concerts of Jullien, and the most unworthy the farragos put on by a certain Professor Anderson, or "The Wizard of the North", to whom the theatre was let in the early months of 1856. This gentleman announced, for Monday, March 3, what he justifiably described as an "extraordinary combination of entertainments", which included "the farce of *The Great Gun Trick*, the opera of *The Sonnambula*, the drama of *Time tries all*, the new squib of *What does he want?*, the melodrama of *Gilderoy*, and the pantomime of *Ye Belle Alliance; or, Harlequin and the Field of the Cloth of Gold*. The carnival", he added, "is to be concluded on Tuesday night by a grand *bal masqué*." According to the dramatist Tom Robertson, who was present, Anderson's *bal masqué* was a miserable affair: "not twenty persons in evening dress, the decorations . . . would have been discreditable to a barn, the company . . . would have disgraced a dancing saloon and only held middle ranks at a penny 'gaff', the whole conduct . . . a disgrace to every one connected with it."

At five minutes to five in the morning of March 5, while the last bars of "God Save the Queen" were bringing this squalid function to a close, the building was discovered to be on fire. Apart from the fact that on this occasion no lives were lost, it was a repetition of the first disaster; by half past five the roof had fallen, and virtually the entire contents of the theatre, including four paintings by Hogarth, were destroyed.

FIRE AT COVENT GARDEN, MARCH 5, 1856
Guests of the Bal Masqué fleeing from the stage
*Engraving from the 'Illustrated London News'*

III

## WITHIN THE MEMORY OF LIVING MEN

HE process of rebuilding took a little longer this time, but not much. During 1857 work proceeded, at Gye's expense and to the designs of Edward Barry, whose father, Sir Charles, built the Reform Club and the Houses of Parliament; immense interest was aroused, and such was the state of chaos right up to the last moment that it seemed impossible that the theatre should reopen its doors on the advertised date of May 15, 1858. It was an age in which gentlemen delighted in laying wagers with one another, and £100,000 was said to have been staked on the event. But the doubters lost; and on the date announced *Les Huguenots* was duly performed, with Grisi and Mario in the principal roles.

It is odd that, despite the intensity of public interest, the house should not have been full; and the proceedings were further marred by disturbances in the gallery. *Les Huguenots* is one of the longest of operas, and by half past midnight the last act had still to come; but the decision to omit it altogether was received, we are told, with "yells and hisses" by "the people of the upper regions". Even "God Save the Queen" failed to silence their protests.

No description is necessary of a theatre whose appearance is still mercifully familiar to us all. The interior is delightful and the acoustics excellent, its one great fault as a theatre being the inadequacy of the foyer, easy circulation in which is impossible when the house is full. It is a great pity that so much of the old site should have been used for the erection of that miniature Crystal Palace, the Floral Hall; in early days concerts used to be given there, but for a long time now its employment has been purely commercial, and the space it occupies is badly needed by the theatre.

For some twenty years the management remained in the hands of Frederick Gye, who pursued his previous policy with little variation. His principal rival was Colonel Mapleson, who gave Italian opera at Her Majesty's until its destruction in 1867, and also at Drury Lane. About this time, too, the languishing cause of English opera took a step forward; every autumn from 1858 to 1864 two capital English singers, Louisa Pyne and William Harrison, rented Covent Garden from Gye, boldly altered its title to "the Royal

AUDIENCE AT COVENT GARDEN
*Engraving from 'Gavarni in London' by Paul Gavarni, 1849*

English Opera", and filled it for several months, performing not only foreign operas translated into English, but also original works by English composers. Though the operas in question—by Balfe, Wallace and Benedict—belong to what is now an impossibly faded tradition, they were nevertheless successful at the time and for long afterwards, and they mark a sort of half-way house in the freeing of English dramatic composition from the tyranny of pastiche and ballad opera. With one of them, Wallace's *Lurline*, Pyne and Harrison are said to have made over £50,000—of which only ten pounds went in performing rights to the composer.

In the summer seasons, Rossini, Bellini and Donizetti were beginning to lose ground to Meyerbeer and Gounod. Gye, who cannot have been much of a musician, went over to Paris in 1863 to hear *Faust*, the great novelty of the day, and came back with the report that there was "nothing much in it but one fine chorus"; as a result of this misjudgement, he lost the honour of its first English production to his rival Mapleson, but he was too good a man of business to admit defeat, and within a month *Faust* was running at both houses; it is a remarkable fact that it remained in the Covent Garden repertory every year without a break from then to 1911.

The year 1861 must be regarded as a watershed in the history of Covent Garden. In that season the beloved Giulia Grisi took her farewell of the stage which she had adorned for so long, and an eighteen-year-old girl named Adelina Patti made an unheralded début of surpassing brilliance; on one dazzling occasion the old and the new luminary appeared together in *Don Giovanni*, as Donna Anna and Zerlina respectively. Since Patti was not only a fabulous singer, but at this period an extremely pretty girl with a particular talent for suggesting the pathetic and the mischievous types of operatic heroine, Gye had reason to consider himself a fortunate man. For all but a few years of the period covered by this chapter, Patti reigned supreme at Covent Garden.

Grisi's no less celebrated husband, the handsome and captivating Mario, continued to sing there for a decade after his wife's departure; but when he too retired, in 1871, it proved by no means so easy to replace him; indeed he left a gap which was never adequately filled, at any of the London opera houses, until the arrival of Jean de Reszke (in his capacity as a tenor) in 1887. The English tenor Sims Reeves, with his sweet tone, natural delivery and perfect execution, might well have occupied the vacant place if the claims of oratorio (and no doubt the snobbishness of the public) had not cut short his operatic career. Another great English singer who never made the name in opera to which his gifts entitled him was the baritone Charles Santley; he attributed his decision to quit the stage for the concert platform to the "lack of earnestness" which made it hopeless to think of getting any honest work done in the opera house.

We have now reached a point in our narrative, just within the memory of living men, at which it becomes worth while to attempt an answer to those most puzzling of questions: what were the performances of the "palmy days" really like, and how would they compare with a typical performance of our own time? Every generation of opera-goers sighs for the memorable singers of the past, and it is therefore tempting to infer that the Golden Age of Opera is a perennial myth, born in the imagination of the old, as they fondly recall the period when they themselves were young, susceptible and uncritical.

There are perhaps two distinct problems here: one concerns the relative prowess of successive generations of individual singers, the other the relative

Zuchelli / Barbiere          1829

ZUCCHELLI, THE BARITONE
As Figaro in 'The Barber of Seville'
*Cartoon by Alfred Edward Chalon, 1829*

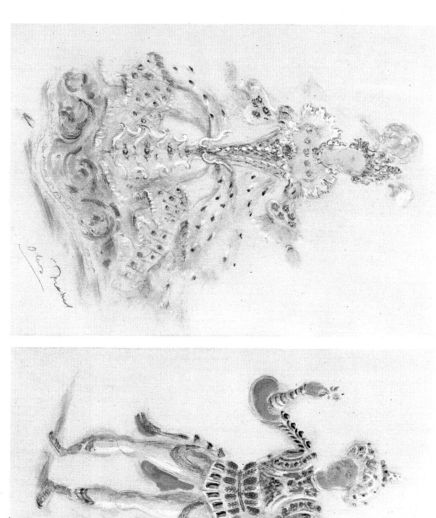

THE PRINCESS AURORA AND A PAGE
Sketches for 'The Sleeping Beauty', performed by the Sadler's Wells Ballet, 1946
Design by Oliver Messel

standard, in different epochs, of the presentation of opera as a whole. Deferring the first problem to a later chapter, when it will be possible to summon the invaluable evidence of the gramophone, let us concentrate our attention for the time being on the second. How were operas performed in their totality? What was the staging like? What standards of rehearsal, ensemble, and attention to the composer's wishes prevailed in an English opera house of the nineteenth century? I think the honest answer must be that in all these respects, which seem so important to us, the standard was extremely low. Costa was certainly a martinet with his orchestra, but not even he—and still less his successors—could make much headway against the lawless doings on the stage. As for the *mise-en-scène*, it is true that one often reads of its "magnificence" or "splendour"; but these words refer to mechanical devices and to lavish expenditure on scene-painting and principals' wardrobes, rather than to a single-minded scenic interpretation of the work as a whole.

But to talk in these terms at all is really an anachronism; the conception of an opera as a unified and inviolable work of art hardly takes shape until the appearance of Wagner. When Mozart and Da Ponte planned *Don Giovanni*, there is nothing to suggest that they regarded themselves as anything but a pair of theatrical craftsmen putting their best work into a commission for a particular place and occasion; if any thought of eternal fame entered their heads, they kept remarkably quiet about it. When the successful Prague *première* was followed by production at Vienna, they thought nothing of writing in a new aria for Donna Elvira, replacing Don Ottavio's taxing "Il mio tesoro" by the simpler "Dalla sua pace", and adding a scene of buffoonery between Zerlina and Leporello which modern taste unanimously condemns. If all this could be done by the composer to his own work, it is hardly surprising to learn of the vicissitudes through which his operas passed in nineteenth-century England; indeed Mozart, who was always writing arias for insertion in other people's operas, must have expected the process to be reversed. Even by the middle of the century, the enormous prestige of Rossini and Meyerbeer could not safeguard these composers from the regular omission of whole acts from their most serious and important productions.

With these considerations in mind, it is worth while to examine a few of the adventures of *Don Giovanni* on the Covent Garden stage during the latter half of the nineteenth century. By 1850 the period of "adaptations" and "additional numbers" *à la* Bishop was past, but the encore nuisance was in full swing: no less than seven numbers were given twice ("Batti batti",

"Vedrai carino", "Il mio tesoro", "Fin ch' han dal vino", "Deh vieni alla finestra", "La cì darem" and the Trio of the Masks), to make up for which Leporello's "Madamina" was not given at all, possibly owing to a last-minute change in the cast. In 1858 the management had the bright idea of casting Mario as Don Giovanni (a baritone part) and the admirable baritone Ronconi as Leporello (a bass); a vagary thanks to which every scene in which either of them appeared had to have its music either transposed or ruthlessly altered. This outrage, one is glad to observe, provoked a good deal of critical comment, and Mario soon resumed the more suitable role of Don Ottavio.

In 1861 we hear of a fairly conscientious performance, with "Mozart's music, all Mozart's music, and nothing but Mozart's music", according to one enthusiastic critic (though I gravely doubt whether the cheerful finale would have been included). In 1865 Santley sang the title role for the first time (at Manchester, as it happens, but with the Covent Garden company); "as usual", he says—and the phrase is worth noting—"*as usual* I had one rehearsal the morning of the day of performance. Mario, who was always a late riser, did not come in until we were half-way through the rehearsal." Perhaps even that should be regarded as an obliging concession on the great tenor's part; Patti had a clause in all her later contracts which absolved her from appearance at any rehearsals whatsoever—and took full advantage of it; so that she occasionally had to be pointed out from the wings to minor artists who had not sung with her before, and were now obliged to accost the unfamiliar *diva* and engage her in a duet.

In 1869 the temporary, and uneasy, amalgamation of the Gye and Mapleson régimes, which resulted from the destruction of Her Majesty's, produced a dazzling *Don Giovanni* cast: Tietjens as Donna Anna, Christine Nilsson as Donna Elvira, Patti as Zerlina, Faure as Don Giovanni and Mario as Don Ottavio. Ravishing sounds, I have no doubt, were heard by the fortunate audience of that season, but there is no suggestion that the standard of presentation or ensemble was any higher than usual. Senseless alterations of the music were freely practised; and Faure is said to have indulged in that hideous high F sharp at the end of the Serenade which can still be heard in a gramophone record by Battistini.

In the 70's and 80's, when the artistic level of Covent Garden dropped to zero, most of the Don Giovannis, according to Bernard Shaw, "swaggered through the part like emancipated billiard-markers"; and the arrival of Augustus Harris in 1888 did more for Meyerbeer and Gounod than for Mozart. In 1889 "Non mi dir" and "Dalla sua pace" were omitted, and the

'DER FREISCHÜTZ': THE WOLF'S GLEN
Signor Maralti as Max, Covent Garden, 1850
*Engraving from the 'Illustrated London News'*

last three scenes appeared totally unrehearsed, so that the stage business went all astray. Two years later more trouble had been taken with the ensemble; but there were still plenty of cuts (Don Giovanni's "Metà di voi", Elvira's "Ah fuggi il traditor", Leporello's "Ah pietà, signori miei", and of course the Finale), and the opera was divided into four acts instead of the two designed by composer and librettist. And so it goes on; even the notable revival of 1926 under Bruno Walter, in which the finale was at last restored, suffered from under-rehearsal, poor stage sets and long waits between the scenes.

The most illuminating and entertaining account of operatic conditions in the mid-nineteenth century is to be found in the two volumes of the *Mapleson Memoirs*. But the Colonel's pleasant sense of humour never allows him to suspect that the anecdotes which he tells so capitally dispose of any serious pretensions on his part to artistic status as an impresario. His rejoinder to such criticism would doubtless be to point out that, compared with others of the same tribe, he was a model of propriety. He might cite as an instance the wonderful E. T. Smith, whom he dissuaded with the greatest difficulty from a scheme for giving "a grand double performance" of *Il Trovatore* at Drury Lane, with the stage divided into two parts as in the last scene of *Aïda*, and a simultaneous performance by two companies, one led by Grisi on the upper floor, and another by Tietjens down below!

I chronicle these absurdities for the sake of historical accuracy, and not at all in order to make merry at the expense of our grandfathers' taste. Every age has its own brand of aesthetic folly, and there are far too many points over which our grandfathers could justifiably turn the tables on us. After all, they did know their *Don Giovanni*, and kept it in the repertory for the greater part of the nineteenth century; which is a great deal more than can be said of ourselves. Nor do I accept the current fashion which depicts audiences of the Victorian and Edwardian ages as so many ignorant snobs, prepared to tolerate anything so long as it was unintelligible. Of course there are people of that sort in every age (in ours they go to the ballet); but it is clear enough, I think, that a fair proportion of the old opera-goers, hearing the world's best singers year after year, developed a limited but perfectly genuine connoisseurship which is in refreshing contrast to the indiscriminate enthusiasms of to-day. Furthermore, they devoted some care to the study of the works which they were about to hear.

A certain Victorian statesman (I forget who) once startled the House by demanding, in the course of some financial debate: "What *is* a pound?" It happened that his son was a young man about town, and *Punch* imagined the reply which might have been made to the parental query:

> A pound, dear father, is the sum
> That clears the opera wicket:
> Two lemon gloves, one lemon ice,
> Libretto, and your ticket.

Note that an evening at the opera was a natural occupation for a young man of fashion; note too that the normal equipment for such an evening included a libretto. Neither assumption is true to-day; nor are modern librettos (when you can get them) a patch on their Victorian predecessors, which were arranged like the Loeb Classics, with the original text on one side and a literal translation on the other, and in some cases "the music of the principal airs" thrown in for good measure. I possess a large collection of these

ADELINA PATTI
*Etching by Pilotelli, c. 1890*

enlightened booklets, some of them bound in leather by the original owner, who has jotted down his impressions of the cast on the pages thoughtfully provided for this purpose by the publishers. Thus on April 3, 1851, Grisi's *Semiramide*, one is not surprised to learn, was considered "glorious", Mme Angri's Arsace is curiously described as "impudent but good", while the Idrenus is briefly dismissed as "a muff".

In the matter of repertory, Mapleson's seasons at Her Majesty's and Drury Lane were often more interesting than those of Gye at Covent Garden. Though he sometimes cast them inadequately, the Colonel did put on works like *Fidelio, Oberon, Iphigénie en Tauride, Zauberflöte, Seraglio*, Spontini's *Vestale* and Cherubini's *Medea*, while Gye frittered away his energies on feeble novelties by such aristocratic nobodies as the Marquis d'Ivry, Prince Poniatowski and the Duke of Saxe-Coburg-Gotha. Both managements fought very shy of Wagner, concerning whose works there was by now the most intense public curiosity; so much so that when Arditi, the composer of *Il Bacio*, conducted the *Götterdämmerung* Funeral March for the first time at a Covent Garden Promenade Concert in the seventies, it was enormously successful and had to be repeated there and then. Nevertheless it was not till 1875 that the twenty-five-year-old *Lohengrin* reached London, and then, characteristically, it was put on by both managements at once—and in Italian too, which was still regarded as the only respectable language for grand opera.

At Covent Garden the first performance lasted till 12.50 a.m.: a fact which is less surprising when one learns that the Italian conductor amiably granted encores, not only of the preludes to Acts I and III, but to a considerable stretch of the concerted scene in the first act which heralds the approach of Lohengrin—though whether the swan was thereby obliged to go into reverse and make a second entrance we are not told. One can well believe Hermann Klein's recollection that the performance was atrocious; nevertheless the public was delighted, and no less so with the novelties of the next season, *Tannhäuser* and *Aïda*. As so often happens, public taste had outstripped that of the managers and the professional musicians, and there is no doubt that the general staleness of the repertory was one of the factors which caused a slump in Italian opera during the 70's and 80's.

The Covent Garden performances of 1877 have been described as "one long exasperation from the first note to the last"; and not even the arrival of new stars of the first order—such as Lassalle (1874), Edouard de Reszke (1880), Sembrich (1880) and Battistini (1883)—could restore the situation. In 1882 both Drury Lane and Her Majesty's ran German opera, the latter including London's first cycles of *The Ring*; next year Carl Rosa began his first and most brilliant period of English opera, producing one or two newly commissioned native works each year. The policy of giving everything in Italian in the grand seasons at Covent Garden came in for severe and justified criticism: reasonable enough in the Rossini-Donizetti period, this practice had lost its point now that so many of the leading singers came from outside Italy and most of the important new operas were either French or German.

Society had for some time ceased to patronise Covent Garden except on Patti nights; and after 1884 Patti herself made only irregular operatic appearances in this country. Her desertion seems to have been the last straw, and Ernest Gye (the husband of the great soprano Albani), who had succeeded his father in 1877, found himself in such difficulties that he had to retire defeated. During the next two or three years spasmodic seasons were given by the irrepressible Mapleson, and by an interesting newcomer named Signor Lago. Lago was obliged to do things very much on the cheap,

COVENT GARDEN: THE THIRD THEATRE
As rebuilt after the fire of 1856
*Engraving from the 'Illustrated London News', 1858*

but he showed great enterprise in the choice of artists and repertory. It was during his various seasons at Covent Garden and elsewhere that he intro-duced to London not only *Orfeo* (and the wonderful Ravogli sisters), the sensational *Cavalleria Rusticana*, and a notable pair of young baritones in D'Andrade and Ancona, but also two of the first Russian operas to be seen in England: Glinka's *Life for the Czar* and Tchaikovsky's *Eugene Onegin*, the latter led by a young conductor named Henry Wood. In 1887 Lago had a rival season at Drury Lane to contend with: a season notable both for the début as a tenor of Jean de Reszke (he had made some fairly successful appearances as a baritone in the seventies) and for the arrival as an im-presario of the young Augustus Harris, son of the Covent Garden stage manager during the régime of Frederick Gye. Harris's move to Covent Garden in the following year begins a new and more brilliant period in the history of the theatre.

## AN AGE OF GREAT SINGERS

N 1888 Augustus Harris was only thirty-six: a young man endowed with a fair amount of musical taste and artistic conscience, and a great deal of enthusiasm and acumen. He perceived that, without a national or municipal subsidy such as is enjoyed by the great Continental opera houses, Covent Garden seasons on a grand scale were possible only with the full support of the fashionable world. In obtaining this he was eminently successful; for many years almost the whole of the two lower tiers of boxes (which in those more aristocratic days swept uninterruptedly around the house) were subscribed in advance for the whole season. This satisfactory situation was due almost entirely to the exertions of two leaders of fashion, Lady Charles Beresford and Lady de Grey (later Marchioness of Ripon); it was thanks to their fondness for opera, their enthusiasm for the brothers De Reszke, and their personal friendship with the Prince and Princess of Wales that Harris was able to ring up the curtain on his first Covent Garden season, on May 14, 1888, with a greater freedom from financial anxiety than any Covent Garden impresario had known for years.

The opera chosen for this occasion was the already somewhat old-fashioned *Lucrezia Borgia*, the only outstanding name in the cast being that of the contralto Zélie Trebelli, then nearing the end of her career. More characteristic of the new order was the début, ten days later, of the Australian soprano Nellie Melba in *Lucia di Lammermoor*; a highly successful occasion, though hardly prophetic of her absolute supremacy at Covent Garden during the next quarter of a century. In June began those joint and several appearances of the two De Reszkes and Lassalle, principally in the works of Gounod and Meyerbeer, which were generally regarded as the gala nights of the Harris régime. Everybody breathed with relief at the disappearance of the worst features which had disgraced the final period of the Gye management; and Covent Garden became not only successful and fashionable once more, but in many respects a fairly satisfactory institution.

By no means, however, in all respects, as was immediately pointed out with ruthless geniality by the most brilliant and entertaining of all musical

SIR AUGUSTUS HARRIS
Surrounded by characters from plays by John Davidson
*Design for a frontispiece by Aubrey Beardsley, 1894*

critics. By a curious coincidence, it was also on May 14, 1888, that the first of a famous series of musical reviews appeared over the pen-name of Corno di Bassetto. Corno di Bassetto was, of course, Bernard Shaw; and for over six years, first in *The Star* and then in *The World*, he coruscated without interruption. It is impossible, half a century later, even when the subject under discussion is as dead as mutton, to open these critiques without reading on and on, and occasionally surrendering to helpless laughter.

Indeed their extreme readability has misled many persons, unaccustomed to associate wit and high spirits with knowledge and taste, to suppose that Shaw was musically ignorant. In truth, however, he was, and is, a thorough musician, and in particular an operatic expert whose memories go back to the mid-seventies, and whose advocacy of Wagner has never blinded him to the beauties of the nineteenth-century Italian repertory—still less to those of his adored Mozart.

Like everybody else, Shaw was fully aware that the Harris régime represented an all-round improvement on the bad old days, and occasionally admitted as much in a critical undertone. But, like Hamlet, he was never content that anything should have been reformed indifferently; his constant cry was: "Oh reform it altogether!" He admits reluctantly that performances of *Werther* with Jean de Reszke and Emma Eames, and of *Roméo et Juliette* with Jean de Reszke and Melba, "seem sure of a place in the front rank of my operatic recollections"; but he never misses an opportunity of ridiculing Harris for failing to put on *Tristan* and *The Ring* with the world's finest tenor in the leading parts. Bayreuth was by now the fashion, but not for years was Shaw's excellent advice taken. In 1892, when Harris wanted to give *The Ring* at Covent Garden, instead of entrusting the work to his own brilliant ensemble, he was obliged to import a complete German company, orchestra and all, conducted by a young man named Gustav Mahler; and in order to please the tenor Alvary, *Siegfried* was actually given first instead of *Rheingold*—an outrage to which one is astonished to learn that Mahler could consent. It was in this season that the word "Italian" was dropped from the name of the Opera House.

Shaw's attacks on the artistic sloth of the De Reszkes gave great offence, especially to their drawing-room patrons; but considering their later Wagnerian triumphs, who can deny that he was right? I have met intelligent friends and pupils of Jean de Reszke who even now cannot tolerate any criticism of their idol, a man of great personal charm as well as a glorious singer. And yet it is difficult not to feel the justification behind Bassetto's good-natured chaff of "Brer Jean" and "Brer Edouard". Hermann Klein, their personal friend and a far less trenchant critic, tells without any malicious intention the story of how, in 1888, he described the Bayreuth *Meistersinger* to the two brothers and Lassalle (who were taking the waters at Bad Ems) in such glowing terms that they insisted first on being *told the plot*, and eventually on going to Bayreuth to see this wonderful novelty for themselves—a "wonderful novelty", be it observed, which was already twenty years old and a popular success in several European capitals! So much

NELLIE MELBA
As Nedda in 'Pagliacci'
*Portrait with autograph on a music cover*

impressed were they by their Bayreuth experience that Jean de Reszke and Lassalle actually got the work up and performed it for Harris next year—in Italian, of course, and with a great many cuts (including the first part of the *Wahnmonolog*!).

It was a tremendous success, and after digesting a great deal of oral and written evidence on the subject, I feel tolerably certain that Jean's Walther von Stolzing must have been the most lyrical and exquisite that has ever been heard; indeed the word "exquisite" is the last that would occur to me in connexion with a single one of the many tenors whom I have heard struggling laboriously through that role. But despite Jean's success as Lohengrin and Walther, it was not until 1896 that he took the long-recommended plunge into Wagner in the original, and added Tristan and Siegfried to his repertoire. Since he retired from Covent Garden altogether in 1900, it was clearly none too soon.

The feature of the Harris régime which inspired Shaw's most hilarious sallies was the absence of all dramatic illusion and the sheer inefficiency of the stage management. In this department too there was no doubt that things had improved; but the future dramatist was not the man to make agreeable concessions. Covent Garden, he constantly complains, had five leading tenors and no stage manager: "for want of a stage manager, no man in *Les Huguenots* knows whether he is a Catholic or a Protestant; and conversations which are pure nonsense except on the supposition that the parties cannot distinguish one another's features in the gloom are conducted in broad moonlight and gaslight." In such conditions no very exalted standard of operatic acting was to be expected; there might be a few individuals of genius such as Giulia Ravogli or Victor Maurel (Verdi's first Iago and Falstaff): but impersonations which passed for profound in their day, like Edouard de Reszke's Mephistopheles, did so only by virtue of a sort of operatic licence.

In 1891 Harris was knighted, not for his services to music, but for happening to be Sheriff of the City of London during the visit of Kaiser Wilhelm II. He was by this time a much overworked man. Carl Rosa's death had left him in charge of the Carl Rosa Company; and though he resigned this position after a year, he took over Drury Lane, bought *The Sunday Times* and even went in for circus management, one Christmas at Covent Garden itself, later on at Olympia. In the midst of this last enterprise, in 1896, death overtook him at the early age of forty-four. Whatever objections might be urged against the other features of his régime, he really did secure for Covent Garden the cream of a very remarkable generation of singers. Look at the list of his *prime donne* for 1895. It is headed by Patti, who after an absence of ten years made six farewell appearances in the roles of Rosina, Violetta and Zerlina (and they were really her last). But the sopranos also included Albani, Sembrich, Melba, Eames, Calvé, Zélie de Lussan and Gemma Bellincioni! Under Maurice Grau, who carried on the Harris traditions for the next five years, the Wagner performances were particularly brilliant. In 1897 *Lohengrin* was sung by the two De Reszkes, Eames, Bispham and Schumann-Heink; in 1898 the De Reszkes appeared in *Tristan* with Milka Ternina, Marie Brema and Anton van Rooy. It is casts such as these which justify old stagers in speaking of the nineties as the last Golden Age of Opera.

JEAN DE RESZKE
As Siegfried
*Drawing by Theobald Chartran, 1896*

And by now we have something better than mere verbal eulogies to judge by, for the gramophone was invented just in time to preserve an impression of the great singers of those days. Jean de Reszke unfortunately disapproved of the only commercial records which were taken of his voice, and refused to allow their publication. Other singers either did not record till they were long past their best, or else failed to do themselves justice in the cramped studios of those days. But, in speaking of these early records, far too much stress is often laid on their technical defects, which actually show in the accompaniments rather than in the voices; without the possibility of flattering electrical amplification, extremely realistic results were often achieved. Mme Emma Eames once listened, in my presence, to a large number of recordings made by her former operatic colleagues; and though she had previously admitted to feeling a prejudice against the gramophone, a few notes were always enough for her to identify the unnamed singer with absolute certainty; of Plançon's *Sonnambula* aria in particular (which was made in 1903) she remarked "It is *exactly* like him; he might be in the room". The best of these old records reveal to an attentive ear a level of vocal excellence unknown to-day: beauty and steadiness of tone, evenness of scale, ease of breath control, and authority of manner.

Among the singers of that date whose superiority over their successors is most evident I count Plançon, Schumann-Heink, Battistini and Lilli Lehmann. The last-named, a frequent Covent Garden visitor about the turn of the century and an early pillar of the Salzburg festivals, deserves a place among the wonders of musical history. To begin with, her versatility was astounding; she sang 165 operatic rôles, ranging from the Queen of the Night and the Forest Bird in *Siegfried* to Carmen, Fricka and Ortrud; among the most famous were Brünhilde, Isolde, Norma, Donna Anna, Constanze (in the *Seraglio*) and Leonora (in *Fidelio*). I have thirty of her recordings, mostly made about 1907 when she was nearly sixty, and including some of the most taxing music ever written for the soprano voice—such things as "Casta Diva", "Ah fors' è lui", "Non mi dir", "Martern aller Arten" and "Abscheulicher! wo eilst du hin?" Of course there are moments when the strain of age is felt; but the sheer technical mastery, and the command of various styles, are such as to put singers of a later day to shame.

The object of this digression has been to answer the question posed in a previous chapter about the relative merit of successive generations of singers. Whatever one may choose to believe about those who flourished long before the advent of the gramophone, the weight of evidence is irresistible that there has been within living memory a landslide in vocal standards—especially when we add to the examples cited above the still more famous names of Melba and Caruso. These two singers must be regarded as the lineal successors of Patti and Jean de Reszke, but they differ in one important respect from the earlier pair. For some obscure reason, Patti never appeared at Covent Garden *with* Jean de Reszke, whereas Melba-Caruso nights were a great feature of the Edwardian period, the most famous vehicle for this combination being Puccini's *La Bohème*. Of course Caruso was in no strict sense a successor of De Reszke, for his style, vocal quality and whole personality were at the furthest remove from those of the elegant Pole; nor did London keep so firm a hold on his services. By this time the Metropolitan was beginning to outbid us, and more than one twentieth-century star, such as Geraldine Farrar and Amelita Galli-

JUBILEE PROGRAMME
For the State Performance, June 23, 1897
*Printed on silk*

Curci, never appeared at Covent Garden at all. The absence of Farrar, the early disappearance from the London scene of Emma Eames, and the infrequent appearances of the popular Austrian soprano Selma Kurz have also been attributed to another cause—the jealousy of Melba; but if there is any truth in this explanation, the *diva* must have been off her guard in the autumn of 1907, when Tetrazzini's limpid flights of *coloratura* burst unheralded upon a half-empty house. She was the most sensational of the Edwardian newcomers, but there are at least two others who must be mentioned even in the briefest chronicle: Antonio Scotti, the suave and sinister Scarpia; and Emmy Destinn, probably the most affecting Aïda, Tosca and Butterfly ever heard at Covent Garden.

Broadly speaking, the policy of the international seasons followed the general lines laid down by Harris, particularly the general principle of performing operas in their original language; but after Grau's retirement in 1902 some relaxation of artistic standards became noticeable. Control passed more and more into the capricious hands of Lady de Grey, whose brother-in-law Henry Higgins shared with Harris's former secretary, Neil Forsyth, the management of the Syndicate; and the limitations of drawing-room taste are evident in the desperately feeble list of novelties produced in the early years of this century. The *Ring* cycles sung in English under Richter in 1908 and 1909 were an outstanding artistic success, but really fresh blood was not pumped into London's operatic veins until Beecham's first season of 1910, when he gave Delius's *Village Romeo and Juliet*, Ethel Smyth's *Wreckers*, and *Elektra*, the first Richard Strauss opera to reach Covent Garden. *Salome* followed in a second Beecham season later in the same year, and his most popular work, *Der Rosenkavalier*, in the spring of 1913.

The sensation of the Coronation Opera Season in 1911 was not operatic at all. During this and the following years, the summer seasons were enlivened by Diaghilev's Russian Ballet, and the impact of this marvellous company on the Western world is perhaps the most significant single artistic event in the first half of our century. Whatever period ought properly to be regarded as the Golden Age of Opera, there can be little doubt that Diaghilev's early seasons, with Nijinsky and Karsavina and the rest in that dazzling chain of masterpieces, *Petrouchka*, *Carnaval*, *Spectre de la Rose* and *Sylphides*, must be considered the Golden Age—at any rate, so far—of Ballet.

The outbreak of the 1914-18 War (during which Covent Garden became a furniture repository) merely drew the curtain across a scene which already showed many symptoms of decline. The gradual loosening of the social hierarchy, the increasing scarcity of great voices, the financial rivalry of America, the movement of public interest away from opera towards orchestral music and ballet, and the unspoken demand for a kind of lyric spectacle more intelligently and artistically produced *as a whole*—all these were pointers to the inevitable end of the drawing-room autocracy of Lady de Grey and "the Smart Set", for whom opera was really a family affair, part of the Season, an occasion to meet one's friends and sigh with audible pleasure over yet another *Roméo* with darling Jean, or yet another Melba-Caruso *Bohème*. The Covent Garden which emerged after the First World War pretended to be the same, but it was different; and the new Covent Garden of our own day has wisely given up all pretence, and accepted the plain truth that times have changed.

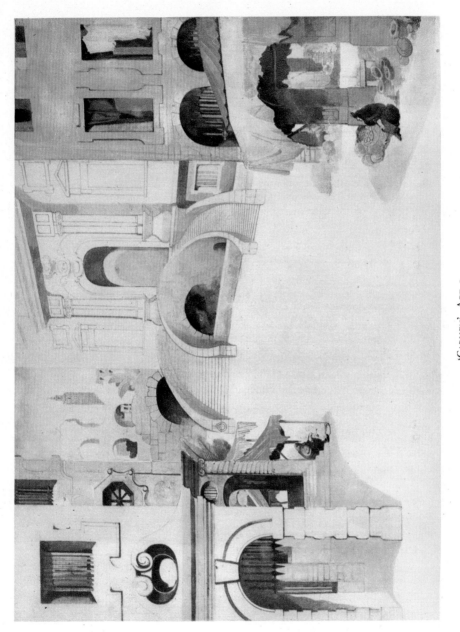

'CARMEN', ACT I

Stage setting for the performance at Covent Garden, 1947

*Design by Edward Burra*

A MANDARIN
Costume design for 'Turandot', Covent Garden, 1947
*Water-colour by Leslie Hurry*

## THE END OF THE STAR SYSTEM

URING the First World War it was Sir Thomas Beecham who kept opera alive in England, and it was he, with invaluable support from Lady Cunard, who played the leading part in its post-war restoration at Covent Garden. The Grand Opera Syndicate had lately suffered a serious loss in the death of their General Manager, Neil Forsyth; and they were doubtless glad to entrust the direction to someone with the operatic experience and enthusiasm of Sir Thomas. He cannot be blamed for the somewhat conventional repertory of the summer seasons of 1919 and 1920, nor for the decline in splendour of the casts : Caruso and Tetrazzini, now nearing the end of their careers, were seen no more; John McCormack had abandoned opera for concert work; Destinn and Martinelli made only a few appearances. Of the old guard the most regular survivor was Melba, her silvery timbre remarkably little touched by the passage of time. There were some charming newcomers, such as the Belgian tenor Fernand Ansseau and the light soprano Graziella Pareto, but they were for the most part of a lesser calibre.

Between these two international seasons the Beecham Opera Company gave autumn and spring English seasons with a much wider repertoire, including *Parsifal*, *Falstaff*, several Russian operas, a certain amount of Mozart, and the *Village Romeo and Juliet* of Delius. The standard of performance was high, and many people thought that if Beecham had abandoned "imported" opera and put all his energies into his English company, a national opera might at long last have been successfully and permanently established. Perhaps he had too many irons in the fire; at any rate the summer season of 1920 pursued its way in an atmosphere of increasing financial anxiety; on the last night of its engagement the Russian Ballet refused to appear, and in September Sir Thomas Beecham was declared bankrupt and the Beecham Opera Company went into voluntary liquidation. Not until 1926 did Sir Thomas return to an active musical career; and not until 1932 did he resume his association with Covent Garden. His bankruptcy was a national as well as a personal misfortune: in the whole course of London operatic history no one had done half so much as he to enlarge and refresh the repertory, or to raise the standard of ensemble and orchestral playing. It is almost incredible to learn that, in the eleven years (four of them war years) from 1909 to 1920, Beecham had produced some 120 operas in all, 60 of them either new to this country or revived after a long period of neglect.

*Après moi*, Sir Thomas might justly have observed, *le déluge*—at any rate, a period of confusion and controversy. The Carl Rosa Company occupied the theatre for two winter seasons; in 1921 there was no summer season at all, and for a time the historic theatre came so far down in the world as to house films and boxing matches. In the two following years, however, the British National Opera Company, which had sprung as a self-governing organisation from the ashes of the Beecham Company, gave both summer and winter seasons at Covent Garden, of which the most ambitious feature was several complete cycles of *The Ring*. In 1924 rival notions as to the proper role of the theatre in our musical life led to a heated public discussion. It was the year of the Wembley Exhibition; and the Syndicate, who were always being asked by their old patrons "when they were going to give us real Grand Opera again", decided that this would be a profitable occasion to invite the famous Vienna Opera Company to visit Covent Garden *en bloc*. This announcement raised a fine flutter, and everybody from the Principal of the R.A.M. to the anonymous "Patron of Opera" aired his views extensively in the press.

The issues were far from simple; as usual, artistic and commercial considerations were hopelessly entangled from the first. The Musicians' Union objected to the importation of foreign musicians, and many serious music-lovers, anxious though they were to hear the Viennese, thought that it was hard luck on the promising but struggling B.N.O.C. to deny them this splendid opportunity of appearing in the "home of English opera". The Syndicate replied that to call Covent Garden the home of English opera was "about as absurd a misrepresentation as could possibly be made"; not only was the theatre private property, but it had been for generations principally the home of foreign opera. In any event, they added, operas *ought* to be sung in the language in which they were written; "that is the right way to produce opera".

On both sides of this perennial dispute there is an immense amount to be said: certainly it admits of no simple and final answer. In 1924 the immediate result of all the fuss was that neither British nor Viennese obtained the theatre; instead, an international season of the traditional type was given. This decision infuriated the extreme partisans of British opera, but it would be puritanical to deny that it brought to the ordinary English opera-goer pleasures more enchanting than any he would otherwise have enjoyed. The 1924 season inaugurated a period of fifteen years in the fortunes of Covent Garden which is the first about which I can write out of my own experience.

Despite all the changes of Syndicate, management and conductors during this period, the pattern set in 1924 remained substantially unchanged; it was a period in which almost all the best performances were German, while the Italian repertory became increasingly slipshod. Bruno Walter, probably the best opera conductor of his day, brought over a contingent of artists who set a standard of all-round accomplishment which had not been known at Covent Garden for many years. No one who began his opera-going career in the twenties can recall without nostalgic emotion the first time he heard the German repertory conducted by Walter, and sung by such artists as Lotte Lehmann, Schumann, Ivogün, Leider, Olszewska, Melchior, Janssen, Bockelmann, Schorr and Kipnis. From constant appearance together, not only in London but in Berlin, Bayreuth and New York, these singers developed an ensemble which went far to remove the objections usually levelled against the "all-star cast". The English orchestra, moreover, re-peating year after year under the same conductors a couple of *Ring* cycles and the other standard masterpieces of Wagner and Strauss, attained a remarkable homogeneity of style.

The years from 1924 to 1939 were beyond question a great period for Wagner, among the greatest London had ever known. As compared with their formidable predecessors, the singers were often deficient in sheer purity and ease of tonal production, and their voices seldom lasted so well. Frida Leider, for example, never possessed the perfect technique of Lilli Lehmann, Milka Ternina or Lillian Nordica; but her Brünhilde and Isolde were none the less expressive, passionately human and marked in particular by a splendid *legato*. In these roles she remained without a serious rival until the appearance, in 1936, of the Norwegian soprano Kirsten Flagstad; and the latter's sheer power and vocal radiance, marvellous as they were in themselves, were felt by some listeners to offer an incomplete compensation for Leider's musicianship and humanity.

The tenor who generally partnered these sopranos was the huge Dane, Lauritz Melchior—huge in every dimension, and the only Wagner tenor of his day whose voice remained fresh at the end of the last act of *Tristan* or *Götterdämmerung*. This capacity, coupled with a highly expressive enunciation of the text, induced musicians to overlook some palpable musical defects: he had only a vague notion of time, and there were few, if any, pages through which he troubled to maintain the exact note values indicated by the composer. The important Wagnerian mezzo-soprano parts of Brangäne, Fricka and Waltraute fell most frequently to that splendid, warm-voiced singer and excellent actress, Maria Olszewska; occasionally to the more statuesque Sigrid Onegin. Herbert Janssen brought to the lighter baritone roles an exceptional beauty of voice and style: his Kurwenal must surely have been among the most touching impersonations ever seen at Covent Garden. In the great bass-baritone parts Friedrich Schorr and Rudolf Bockelmann divided our allegiance pretty evenly; the majestic voice of Schorr contained a dictatorial note which made him a most impressive Wotan, while Bockelmann was perhaps the more serene and mellow Hans Sachs of the two. Among the many fine basses Otto Helgers and Alexander Kipnis were outstanding.

But perhaps the most enchanting of all the singers who visited us regularly between the wars was Lotte Lehmann. She had sung the part of Sophie in *Der Rosenkavalier* at Drury Lane in 1913, but her real London career dates from 1924. A whole generation can scarcely think of the parts of Elsa or Eva or Sieglinde without the luscious quality of Lehmann's voice and the urgency and warmth of her marvellous diction. How many of her phrases haunt one still!—among them, Eva's question about her lover's performance in the singing school, "Sang er so schlecht, so fehlervoll?" (who can forget the way she used to *breathe out* those consonants in her anxiety?); or the great outburst of emotion in the third act beginning "O Sachs! Mein Freund! Du teurer Mann!" And how many more such moments there were in *Fidelio* and *Rosenkavalier*!

Fine as were the Wagner performances of these years, one can easily see that in certain respects they must have fallen short of past attainments; indeed, in the instance of Jean de Reszke and his successors, the case hardly requires proving. It is on the other hand extremely difficult to believe that better performances of *Der Rosenkavalier* can ever have been given anywhere than those of the twenties and early thirties at Covent Garden. It was sung there time and again by the same ideal cast, until it began to seem as though Strauss himself must have had the very timbre and intonations of these voices in mind when composing the music, though none of them had in fact taken part in the Dresden *première*. The Marschallin was Lotte Lehmann's greatest part; "the lyric stage of the time", wrote Richard Capell in *Grove's Dictionary*, "knew no performance more admirably accomplished; it seemed to embody a civilisation, the pride and elegance of old Vienna, its voluptuousness, chastened by good manners, its doomed beauty." From this

LOTTE LEHMANN
As the Marschallin in 'Der Rosenkavalier'
*Photograph by Ellinger, Salzburg*

wonderful impersonation everyone has doubtless compiled his own nostalgic anthology: the famous aristocratic curl of the lip with which she commented on the departure of Baron Ochs—"Da geht er hin, der aufgeblasne, schlechte Kerl"; the intimate, varied, laughing ease of the series of conversations with Oktavian; the immense dignity and distinction of her appearance in the last act; the opening phrase of the trio; the final humorous-tragic "Ja, ja" with which, on Faninal's arm, she left behind the young lovers—and her own youth.

As for those lovers—Elisabeth Schumann was the Sophie of one's dreams; no one else came near her in those long soaring phrases with which she acknowledged the gift of the silver rose; "exquisite" is an overworked word, but nothing else will do for that long, fine-drawn thread of sound, those ravishing *pianissimo* high notes at "Wie himmlische, nicht irdische, wie Rosen vom hochheiligen Paradies". None of the various Oktavians proved quite so inevitable a choice as that: Delia Reinhardt was probably the best of the early years, Tiana Lemnitz of those who sang the part in the late thirties—but by then the remainder of the classic cast had been broken up. As for the Baron Ochs, there could never be any doubt during the lifetime of Richard Mayr. The Strauss-Hofmannsthal correspondence shows that this wonderful native of Salzburg was in the composer's mind from the first, and Mayr filled out the part with a wealth of detail, a gusto and a virtuosity, that were truly inimitable. One remembers him in the first act, sitting at his ease in the Marschallin's bedroom, pouring out a stream of scandalous gossip in that over-ripe Viennese dialect of which he was a master; he never seemed to glance at the conductor, or to trouble his head with such details as bar-lines and rests and cues; it might have been a bravura speech from some play by Sheridan—and yet every note was impeccably there. I shall never forget the first impact of this apparently careless display: it was a revelation of what acting in the opera house can be.

Yes, those were wonderful *Rosenkavaliers*, the like of which I don't expect to hear or see again. Fortunately their purely musical virtues are not, for once, a mere matter of dogmatic assertion on the one side and polite incredulity on the other, since there exists a gramophone album of more or less substantial selections sung by Olszewska (a rather too feminine Oktavian), Schumann, Lehmann and Mayr. But there were many other great occasions in those inter-war years besides Wagner and *Der Rosenkavalier*. *Fidelio* I have already mentioned; there was an *Ariadne auf Naxos* with Lehmann, Schumann and that most delicate *coloratura* Maria Ivogün; and there was Bruno Walter's unforgettably swagger *Fledermaus* with Lehmann as the sentimental Rosalinde, and Schumann as the lively Adele. In spite of Elisabeth Schumann, it was not on the whole a great Mozart period. To begin with, there was the language difficulty: nobody was pleased when *Figaro* was sung in German; and a strong *Don Giovanni* cast, for which Leider, Lehmann and Schumann had specially learned their parts in Italian, obviously needed more rehearsal and more careful production than were possible in the circumstances.

Not much help was to be expected from Italy. Italians have seldom excelled in Mozart; and even in their own music it was evident that Italian singing had entered a period of decline. After the Germans had gone, a feeling of slackness invaded the house. The weather was perhaps hotter; the orchestra, exhausted by the demands of Wagner and Strauss, were inclined to take it easy with Verdi and Puccini. Singers did as they pleased, and what they pleased to do was often deplorable: opera-goers still speak with bated

RICHARD MAYR
As Baron Ochs in 'Der Rosenkavalier'
*Photograph by F. F. Bauer, Munich*

breath of the horrors of the *Ugonotti* of 1927 or the *Don Carlo* of 1933. Many
of the best performances given in Italian opera in these years were not by
Italians at all. Best of all, perhaps, was the Aïda of Elisabeth Rethberg
(to the Amneris of Olszewska); but our own Eva Turner was a notable
exponent of the same part, and an incomparable Turandot. I remember
also the Norwegian Eide Norena in a very fine performance of *Otello* (with
Martinelli and Lawrence Tibbett) in 1938; and many years before, Lotte
Lehmann contributed a Desdemona (with Zenatello as Otello) which I
cannot console myself for having missed; it was this performance which
prompted an Italian singer to utter the naïve congratulation which caused
so much amusement behind the scenes: "Brava, madame! You sing just
like an Italian!"

But it is time to speak of the better Italians, or I, who have an absolute
hunger for *bel canto*, shall find myself accused of an anti-Italian bias! Let us

begin by counting as honorary Italians those two fine artists Rosa Ponselle and Conchita Supervia, though the one is a citizen of America and the other was a native of Spain. In both, beauty and immense stage charm accompanied an unusual faculty of investing the older florid music with its true dramatic significance; in honour of Rosa Ponselle (a fascinatingly unconventional Violetta) Bellini's *Norma* was successfully revived; and for Conchita Supervia those delicious and still rarer comic operas of Rossini, *La Cenerentola* and *L'Italiana in Algeri*, which might have been specially written for her extraordinary *coloratura* contralto. In Rossini's day the florid passages were doubtless more smoothly sung than by Mme Supervia, but the roles can never have been given with a more captivating *brio* or a more mischievous wit; and she might still be singing them to-day had she not died in 1936, at the very height of her fame.

Among her partners in these welcome Rossini revivals was the fine *basso cantante* Ezio Pinza; overwhelmingly ripe as the Rossinian equivalent of Baron Hardup, he excelled no less in serious roles, the only pity being that the bass parts in Italian opera are so much less interesting and important than those written by German or Russian composers. Mozart's Don Giovanni really lay too high for his voice, but he made a fine thing of it all the same. That accomplished *buffo* baritone Mariano Stabile created a great impression as Gianni Schicchi, and a greater still as Falstaff, a part in which he has no contemporary rivals; and a justly famous representative of the old school, Giuseppe de Luca, made a single (and totally unheralded) appearance in 1935 as Figaro in the *Barbiere;* his voice had by then lost its power but not its smoothness and flexibility, and his style might well have served as a model to the greatly gifted but artistically naïve Lily Pons, who sang with him as Rosina. More satisfactory exponents of such *coloratura* soprano parts were Toti dal Monte and Lina Pagliughi, but like so many of the better Italian singers, their appearances at Covent Garden were all too infrequent and one usually had to put up with inferior substitutes.

The various syndicates and managements which succeeded one another seemed unable to achieve anything like the same continuity in the Italian sphere as in the German. Lack of enterprise may have accounted for such things as the absence of Martinelli from 1919 to 1937, and it is difficult to understand the total failure to engage that most delicate of Italian tenors, Tito Schipa; but the infrequent appearances of Gigli (in three seasons only) were simply due to our inability to pay the price demanded by a star whose performances were expected to bring him in some £50,000 a year.

A paradox among tenors was Beniamino Gigli; a "strange harmony of

ELISABETH SCHUMANN
As Sophie in 'Der Rosenkavalier'
*Photograph by Setzer, Vienna*

contrast", to quote Puccini's translator. On the one hand a divine voice,
certainly the greatest since Caruso (though of a lighter calibre), an admirable
(not quite ideally flexible) technique, and an immense gusto, vivacity and
charm; on the other hand sobs, gulps, exaggerated *portamenti*, street-corner
vulgarities which could reduce the sensitive listener in a moment from
ecstasy to despair. Gigli represented at once the virtues and the vices of
the star system; a contrast which was still more noticeable in the Covent
Garden appearances of the magnificent Russian bass Chaliapin. These were
inevitably less satisfactory to musicians than the fabulous 1913 and 1914
seasons at Drury Lane, or even than his Lyceum season of 1936 (although
by then his voice was past its best), because on those occasions he was
surrounded by a Russian company. At Covent Garden, either he sang *Boris
Godunov* in Russian while the rest of the company sang it in Italian or near-
Italian; or he would invest such French and Italian parts as Leporello,

Basilio or Mephistopheles with a startling, but somewhat alien, sort of brilliance, and in doing so impose his will ruthlessly on the unfortunate conductor.

Such polyglot performances of *Boris* were a survival of the irrational eccentricities of the past, and a similar anomaly occurred on one or two occasions when Melba gave her services to help the B.N.O.C. and sang an Italian Mimi amid a group of British Bohemians. Her farewell to Covent Garden exemplified another tradition which had frequently marked such occasions—and also Command Performances—in the past: the practice of giving single acts from different operas on the same night. On June 8, 1926, she sang the second act of *Roméo*, the last of *Otello* (as far as the entry of the Moor) and the third and fourth of *La Bohème*; the programme, it was observed, might have been devised so as to include the words "Adieu" and "Addio" as often as possible. Electrical recording had just been invented in time to preserve the occasion and to demonstrate for ever how much purity and steadiness of tone a singer can command in her sixty-eighth year, provided that her vocal method is absolutely perfect. An era of operatic history seems to have been ended by the departure of Melba and the death, in 1928, of Harry Higgins, that genial hoarse-voiced impresario who is the subject of so many anecdotes. Once, it is said, Higgins was negotiating with a soprano more famous for her personal beauty than for her voice; when she named a preposterous fee, "Dear lady," he whispered in his confidential croak, "we're only asking you to *sing!*"

I have treated the 1924-1939 period as a whole, delving haphazard into my own memories of it rather than attempting to follow the various changes of management and syndicate. The principal break occurred in 1933, when Colonel Eustace Blois, who had been Managing Director for several years, died and was succeeded by Sir Thomas Beecham, whose supremacy lasted until 1939. But the system established by Bruno Walter, Colonel Blois and Mrs. Courtauld in the twenties (a month of German opera in May, followed by about the same, or rather less, of Italian with a sprinkling of French) remained substantially unchanged, except that it became the custom to follow the opera season by an increasingly prolonged season of Russian ballet. Though those who remembered the great days of Diaghilev might be disappointed, there were always plenty of new ballets, and even of new *kinds* of ballet (such as Massine's symphonic experiments); but the opera repertory was sadly unadventurous. The most startling and memorable of the Beecham performances was perhaps the *Elektra* (with Rose Pauly) of 1938. Strauss himself came over with the entire Dresden company in the

'DER ROSENKAVALIER', ACT I
Stage design for post-war production, April 1947
*By Robin Ironside*

winter of 1936 (a visit much criticised on political grounds), and conducted his *Ariadne auf Naxos*, in which I heard the prodigious rather than beautiful voice of Erna Sack touch the incredible note of B *in altissimo*: allowing for the intervening rise in pitch, it was the same note as the *c''''* reached by Lucrezia Agujari to the astonishment of Mozart. During the Coronation Season of the following year the Paris Opera company brought over, among other works, Gluck's *Alceste* and Dukas's *Ariane et Barbe-Bleue*, in both of which Germaine Lubin made a great success. English seasons were sometimes given in the autumn, but new or newly performed English operas, whether by Goossens, Delius, Coates or Lloyd, never proved successful enough to find a place in the permanent repertory.

Great as were the pleasures provided by the best performances of these fifteen years, it must be said that the system neither encouraged the growth of native opera nor kept us abreast of the vital novelties of the Continent. None of the main operatic currents of Europe reached our shores; we participated in neither the Handel nor the Verdi renaissance (indeed one of Verdi's finest works, *Simon Boccanegra*, has never yet been performed in England); none of the operas of Respighi or the more recent successes of

THE PRINCESS TURANDOT
Design for Eva Turner's costume, July 1947
*By Leslie Hurry*

Wolf-Ferrari was given; and London had to be content with concert performances of Busoni's *Doktor Faust*, Shostakovich's *Lady Macbeth of Mtsensk*, Hindemith's *Mathis der Maler* and Berg's *Wozzeck*.

The Syndicates could not be fairly blamed for their cautious policy; they had to make both ends meet. In 1930, it is true, the Labour Government took the historic step of granting a small subsidy, paid through the Postmaster-General and the B.B.C.; but this naturally became one of the first victims of the National Government's policy of "retrenchment". Summer seasons tended to get shorter, until in 1939 there were only six weeks of opera; every now and then we were told that the beloved old theatre was about to be pulled down. At this recurrent threat music-lovers were invariably sad, and often angry; but it was hopeless to expect the National Government to intervene in a matter touching private property, and all that could be done was to sit still and hope for the best. What happened in 1939 could hardly be described as the best; but so far as Covent Garden was concerned it might have been a great deal worse.

VI

## THE PROSPECT BEFORE US

EGRADED to a furniture depository during the First World War, Covent Garden enjoyed this time a fate more cheerful, if no more appropriate. Like an elderly *prima donna* who obliges at a NAAFI concert with a spirited performance of "Tipperary", the dear old theatre "did its bit" by accepting the role of a commercial dance hall, highly popular with the armed forces on leave. In the last year of the war, the musical public was much relieved to learn that Messrs. Boosey & Hawkes (the well-known firm of music publishers) had taken a five years' lease of the house, with the intention of restoring it to its proper function as the national home of opera and ballet.

As so often happens in England, the Government began cautiously to support what private enterprise had initiated. A body known as the Covent Garden Opera Trust was formed, working in association with the Arts Council, and having for its first chairman Lord Keynes, who was also Chairman of the Arts Council; after his untimely death in 1946, he was succeeded by Sir John Anderson. The administration of the theatre was placed in the hands of David Webster, who during the war had managed the affairs of the Liverpool Philharmonic Society with conspicuous success.

To create a National Lyric Theatre from scratch within a year or two is an unenviable task, and the Trust did well at the outset to persuade the justly admired Sadler's Wells Ballet to migrate *en masse* to Covent Garden, bringing with them their director Ninette de Valois, their principal choreographer Frederick Ashton and their conductor Constant Lambert, and leaving a vigorous junior establishment behind them at Sadler's Wells. On February 20, 1946, the Royal Opera House was reopened, in the presence of the King and Queen, with a newly mounted full-length performance of Tchaikovsky's sumptuous ballet *The Sleeping Beauty*, in which the leading parts were danced by Margot Fonteyn and Robert Helpmann. It was a happy choice: not only was the dancing accomplished and Oliver Messel's décor brilliant, but the fable itself seemed strangely appropriate to the occasion. Was not the theatre itself the real Sleeping Beauty, newly re-awakened and handsomely restored to life, with its great red velvet curtains, its elegant clusters of pink-shaded candles and its ceiling of pistachio green? Here at any rate, the audience seemed to feel that night, was one beautiful thing which had survived the war, to all appearances unchanged.

Change, however, there has been; not so much in the physical aspect of the house (though a few more boxes have gone) as in the matter of policy. The bulk of the year's entertainment is now provided from our own resources, the Sadler's Wells Ballet alternating with a native opera company singing in English. Foreign opera is not wholly excluded, but it must take the form of short seasons given by complete visiting companies. It was one of these, a Neapolitan troupe, which gave Covent Garden (on September 9, 1946) its first post-war operatic performance, Verdi's *La Traviata*. Margherita Carosio made a touching Violetta; the remainder of the company was undistinguished except for a young baritone named Paolo Silveri, and its repertory was confined to the usual cast-iron successes; but the performances were at least vital and full-blooded, and audiences, in their pleasure at hearing "the real thing" again, were not disposed to be too critical. A year later, the Vienna State Opera, together with the incomparable Vienna Philharmonic Orchestra, presented balanced and stylish performances of Mozart's three buffo operas, of *Fidelio*, and of *Salome*, in which Ljuba Welitsch gave a striking and beautifully sung impersonation of the Strauss heroine. There were welcome visits also from the American Ballet Theatre and the De Basil company; but nothing in this field proved more exhilarating than the return, as a guest with our own company, of Léonide Massine. This great dancer and choreographer not only danced his old roles in *Le Tricorne* and *La Boutique Fantasque* with a carcely diminished *brio*, but himself directed these spirited revivals and the first English production of his latest work, *Mam'zelle Angot*.

Meanwhile the new opera company was getting into its stride under the direction of Karl Rankl, an Austrian conductor resident in England. A revival of Purcell's masque *The Fairy Queen* formed a kind of stepping stone between ballet and opera; in January 1947 *Carmen* was produced, followed by several other revivals of standard works which soon revealed both the strength and the weakness of the new dispensation. The performances were, for the most part, well rehearsed, the orchestra fair, the chorus excellent; and it was an agreeable surprise to find the designs entrusted, no longer to an anonymous scene-painter, but to artists of some repute. The great difficulty so far has been to find solo singers capable of sustaining the leading roles in so large a house. For the second season a compromise was adopted, and a few foreign singers, among them Flagstad and Silveri, were invited to strengthen the domestic company as guests. It was probably, in the circumstances, a prudent decision.

The artistic sins and absurdities of the old operatic régime have not been minimised in the course of this narrative. In former days almost everything was sacrificed to the singers, and now perhaps the pendulum has swung too far in the opposite direction. It is important, certainly, to have good lighting, production and décor; still more so to provide a first-class orchestra and chorus; but none of these virtues will reconcile the public for long to singers with clumsy technique, poor style and indifferent tone. Opera is a composite art, and one of its principal attractions has always been the thrill of a great voice greatly used. This is a truth which no opera house in the world can safely neglect; least of all Covent Garden, which has been for a hundred years the home of the greatest singing in the world.

'LES RENDEZVOUS'
Sketch for costumes: Margot Fonteyn and corps de ballet
*By William Chappell*

# INDEX

(The figures in italics refer to the pag s on which illustrations appear)